Sea's
A Tale from
Nigeria

Retold by Donna Latham
Illustrated by Pamela Becker

Scott Foresman
is an imprint of

Glenview, Illinois • Boston, Massachusetts • Chandler, Arizona •
Upper Saddle River, New Jersey

Illustrations
Pamela Becker.

Photographs
Every effort has been made to secure permission and provide appropriate credit for photographic material. The publisher deeply regrets any omission and pledges to correct errors called to its attention in subsequent editions.

Unless otherwise acknowledged, all photographs are the property of Pearson Education, Inc.

22 NASA.

ISBN 13: 978-0-328-52673-4
ISBN 10:   0-328-52673-8

3 4 5 6 7 V0FL 17 16 15 14 13 12

Long, long ago when the world was new, Sun and Moon lived on Earth. Though they were brother and sister and the best of friends, Sun and Moon were as different as, well, day and night. In fact, they had only one thing in common: they shared the most popular hut in the village.

What made brother and sister so different? Well, Sun with his round beaming face and rosy cheeks loved to roam the hills and wander the valleys. As he strolled over the land's expanse, always laughing and smiling, merry Sun greeted all the people he met and brightened their days.

Wherever Sun traveled, people of all ages and walks of life flocked around him. They laughed at his silly jokes and basked in the warmth of his sunny spirit and radiant smile. Being surrounded by friends caused Sun's round face to glow all the brighter.

"My hut may be tiny," Sun told everyone he met, "but the door is always open. All are welcome. Promise you'll visit me soon!"

Sun and Moon's home was just that—a tiny hut with its door forever ajar, filled with the constant flow of friends who would chat and play music at all hours of the day and night. It was the place to be, and Sun was its popular social center.

Moon, in contrast, was quiet and shy. Her crescent-shaped face always looked serious and deep in thought.

She had kind eyes that matched her kind manner. Moon didn't enjoy attention or chit-chatting with friends; she craved solitude and seldom ventured far from home.

When Sun entertained his noisy pals, Moon slipped outside their cramped hut and wandered down the hillside. She lay in soft grasses with her fingers clasped behind her head. Feeling at peace in the silence, Moon gazed at glittering stars for hours, enjoying their soundless company. She was glad to have escaped the din of Sun and his friends' ceaseless chatter.

One glorious morning, Sun approached Moon in her garden and announced his latest idea. Sun shone with an extra brightness, as he always did when he was thinking of new things.

"This tiny hut has become way too crowded," he announced. "It's time to build a larger one."

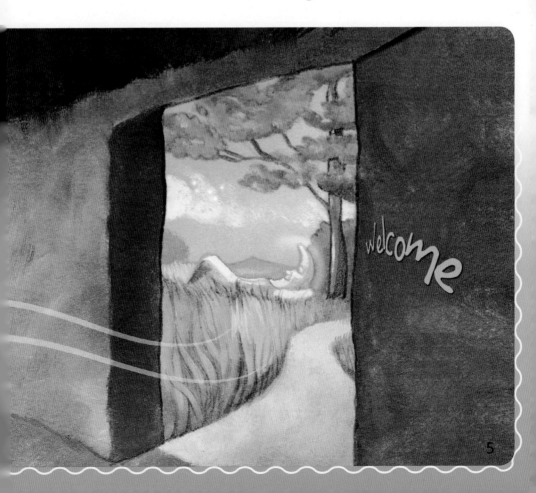

Moon got to her feet. "Let's not be greedy," she warned. "Why do we need a bigger hut?"

"So I can invite more friends to visit. I'll be the most popular person in the land." He beamed even more brightly at this thought.

Moon didn't want more visitors—or a new home for that matter. But knowing Sun would eventually get his way, she caved saying, "As long as our new home can have a hatch in the roof so that I can see the sky . . ."

Barely listening, Sun had already turned his back to her as he cut off his sister mid-sentence. "Sure, sure of course, and we'll anchor the hut high on the hilltop."

Brother and sister shook hands and agreed to start working on their new home right away.

Sun and Moon ventured through the densest areas of the forest. They chopped down hollow bamboo stems.

They gathered palm fronds for the hut's roof.

Arms full of bamboo and fronds, they headed to the hilltop. "I'll weave the thatched roof and build bamboo eaves," said Moon. She was an excellent planner. She always helped Sun bring his ideas to life. "You tackle the floor and walls."

"This hilltop is perfect," Sun said as he bound together sturdy bamboo poles to form a platform.

"Because we are closer to the stars I love?" Moon asked. Her brother's thoughtfulness caused her narrow face to break into a wide grin. *He's so kind to remember my wishes,* she thought.

"Not exactly," Sun admitted slowly. Orange patches covered his cheeks as he worked in the heat. "From our hilltop, we can see all the way across the grassy lowlands."

Moon's smile shriveled like a flower without water. "And . . . ?"

"Here, we have a clear view of Sea. She lives where the land ends. Look!" Sun pointed to Sea in the distance.

"Bah!" Moon grumbled. "You chatter on and on about Sea. Sea this and Sea that. Sea, Sea, Sea." Suddenly annoyed at Sun, Moon worked faster.

"Sea is my dearest friend," Sun replied. He had no idea why his sister was getting so worked up.

Moon stopped working, took a deep breath, and looked at Sun. She put her hands on her hips and in a pained voice said, "Oh, *really*?"

Jealousy rumbled in Moon's belly like a waking volcano. She jutted out her pointed chin. The shadowy hollows in her cheeks grew dark. "I thought *I* was your best friend."

Sun beamed. "You are, you are, dear sister. But Sea is also precious to me."

"Then why doesn't she ever visit you? *Hmm?* You ramble over the land to visit Sea every single day. She never, ever returns the favor." Moon stood steady in her stance.

Sun's round face grew dim. "Well, um . . ." He didn't know how to respond to his sister's question. Suddenly he didn't want to talk about Sea any longer. Moon continued staring at him, and Sun felt a pang of doubt. In an attempt to change the subject, he asked, "How's the roof coming?"

"Um," Moon said as she looked down at her incomplete work. Without realizing what she was doing, she sat back down and again began to weave fronds in tight rows with her nimble fingers.

"Ta-da!" Moon cried. "It's sure to keep out pouring rains and wriggly tarantulas." Sun had successfully distracted her. Looking proud, Moon indicated the narrow hatch she had woven into the roof.

"What's that for?" asked Sun, looking where she was pointing.

"When I yearn to gaze at the stars after we are snug in our beds, I can throw open the hatch and peek outside," Moon said, instantly forgetting their conversation about, and her jealousy over, Sun's friend Sea. But Sun had not forgotten.

"Huh!" Sun snorted. Moon's earlier words still stung his heart, causing him to flash with anger. "You yammer on and on about the twinkling stars. Stars this and stars that. Stars, stars, stars."

"At least my glittering friends visit me," Moon sneered. "Not like your oh-so-mysterious Sea. She never shows her precious face around here."

Sun's mouth hung open and then quickly clamped shut, for he had no response to her jeer. That night, Sun tossed and turned. Moon's words made him reflect on his friendship with Sea.

"Moon's right. Sea never pays me a visit," he sighed. "What kind of a friend is that?" And the more he thought about it, the more heated up with anger he grew.

Finally morning came, and Sun jumped from his bed. With long strides, he journeyed over the hills. He roamed over the grassy lowlands. Finally, he reached where the land ended and met the water. He could see his friend Sea waiting for him; she was a wondrous sight—her face draped in seaweed, her eyelashes fluttering, and her long arms floating in the crystal blue of her watery body.

Sea saw Sun approaching from a distance—a sight that always made her smile. She waited patiently, as her waves gently rocked against the sandy shore: slosh, slosh, slosh.

"Sun, my friend," Sea called. "Why did you not visit me yesterday?"

"Sea, we must talk," Sun said, ignoring her question. He stood with hands clenched at his sides.

"Why so serious?" Sea burbled with laughter. "Your face is cloudy." Her seaweed hair fluttered around her face. Her slender arms rose and fell in her waves.

"Sea, you never visit me. I daily wander a great distance to chat with you. Yet, you never come to my hut."

"Oh, Sun!" Sea cried. "I would love to visit your home," she said wistfully. "But behold my vastness! I'm endless, don't you see? I'd never fit inside your hut!"

"My sister Moon and I have built a bigger hut, high on a hilltop," Sun boasted. "Now, there's plenty of room for all my friends, including my favorite friend, you!"

I am not leaving until Sea agrees to visit our hut, Sun thought stubbornly.

Sea was flattered, but concerned. "Perhaps," she said thoughtfully. "But is there room for all of *my* friends?" Sea raised her azure eyebrows. "Where I go, my many friends must follow."

Sun beamed. "The more the merrier!"

"Sun, are you sure? You should know that . . ."

"Sure!" he interrupted.

After a moment's hesitation, Sea cried, "Then, lead the way! Let's surprise Moon."

Sun dashed excitedly through the lowlands and over the hills. He raced toward his hut high on the hilltop. Behind him, Sea followed with her waves rising and falling: slosh, slosh, slosh.

Back at the hut, Moon was tending the yam plants in the garden she'd planted around their new hut. She enjoyed the solitary work. Moisture gathered on her cheeks, and she dabbed it away with the back of her hand.

A sharp, salty scent grew in the air. In the distance, a gentle sloshing sound was washing over the hills. Moon looked up, puzzled.

"Moon, Moon!" Sun, running up the hill, waved joyously. "I have a surprise—a huge surprise—for you." Sun's round face glowed. "Meet my friend, Sea."

Moon stood up and watched as a narrow stream trailed behind Sun. The salty smell began to increase,

as the stream quickly approached. Moisture hung more heavily in the air. Moon felt a sudden pang of anxiety; she wasn't sure whether it was the anticipation of her brother's friend finally visiting their hut or something else entirely. However, she dismissed the feeling and greeted Sea warmly.

"Hello, Sea," said Moon.

"Greetings!" called Sea in return. Until the rest of her body arrived, she was only a shallow stream; she hardly looked like herself.

Water encircled the yam plants. Moving faster, it swooshed around Moon's ankles. Sun lifted one foot and dipped his toes in the cool stream.

"Please, come inside," said Moon as she opened the door of the hut. Sea flowed inside. A starfish and a sea anemone, waving its tentacles, followed.

"I hope you don't mind, but I've brought my friends," Sea said. "All of them, whether they have fins, fur, or feathers."

The land beneath their feet rocked. Crash, crash, crash; waves pounded against the hillside and the sides of the hut as Sea's body continued to flow inside. Water rose to Moon's knees, and still it came. All day, until evening, Sea flowed into the hut.

"Moon!" Sun called. "Isn't this wonderful? I'm the most popular person in the village."

Seabirds rode Sea's waves, while turtles and fish swam beneath them. Crabs and lobsters scuttled under Sea and clicked their claws to greet Moon. Playful seals dove beneath Sun's feet, and dolphins somersaulted over his head.

Sun beamed. He played in the rippling water with Sea's friends. Sea was delighted, too, knowing she was making her friend happy.

But Moon was neither happy nor delighted. Waist-deep in frothy waves, Moon worried. "Sun," she called. "Our hut is too small for all of Sea's friends."

"The more the merrier!" Sun yelled. He splashed his sister playfully and laughed.

Noticing the worried look on Moon's face, Sea looked around: she and her friends were flowing through every nook and cranny of the large hut. Now she, too, was worried.

One of Sea's waves crashed against Moon. Moon tumbled headfirst into the water as her feet went up over her head. And yet, higher and higher the water level rose. A wild wave grabbed Sun and swirled him toward the thatched roof. At last, Sun also grew anxious.

Sea yelled to Sun, "I'm so sorry. I should have known this would happen, but you were so insistent on my visiting . . ." Sun no longer cared about his popularity or having visitors in his hut; he was now only worried about his sister's safety and his own.

"Moon," Sun cried. "I'm in over my head! Sea has overwhelmed our hut. How can we escape?"

Moon gulped air and dove beneath the waves. She reached her brother, seized his arm, and swam with him to the other end of the hut.

She threw open the hatch in the thatched roof and pushed Sun through it. Then he turned and helped as Moon scrambled outside herself.

Sun and Moon climbed up over the eaves. They perched at the very tip of the roof. As they peered down, they saw an enormous whale riding the waves toward their hut. Sun covered his eyes.

"Look what I've caused," Sun moaned. "With her vastness and her many friends, Sea has overtaken our new home. There's no place to seek shelter. Oh, I never should have invited her here . . ." Sun let out a long sigh.

"My jealousy caused me to provoke you," Moon said. "I'm so very sorry we quarreled."

To comfort her brother, Moon reached out and clasped Sun's hand. Sun put his head on his sister's shoulder. Moon then glanced up at the black sky, where countless stars twinkled.

Moon turned to her brother. "I have a crazy idea," she said in a serious tone. "Maybe we need something *more* than a hut." Sun looked bewildered.

Moon continued. "I don't think we could build a hut big enough for all your friends to visit. And seeing your friends is what makes you happiest."

Sun nodded in agreement. "But, Moon, where could we go where I could see all my friends all the time?"

"I know just the place."

Then Moon tightened her hand around her brother's and leaped as high as she could. Together they floated high into the sky. She positioned Sun directly above the land and Sea.

"Sun," Moon said. "You love your friends, so radiate your warmth and light over them each day. They will wake up every morning to your shining face." Sun smiled; he liked this idea.

"But where will *you* go?" Sun asked.

"As you know, I adore peace and quiet. I will enjoy the land and Sea at night, when the world is at rest." She drifted away from Sun. "I'll take my turn first."

"Wait," said Sun. "We've never been apart."

"And we never will be." Moon smiled, and the hollows in her cheeks flickered. "There's plenty of room in the sky for both of us."

And to this very day, Sun and Moon live in the sky above the land and Sea, the brother watching over the day and the sister over the night.

21

The Blue Marble

Did you know that NASA nicknamed Earth the Blue Marble? In 1972 the crew of Apollo 17, hurtling through space, snapped a stunning photo. With whirls of white, dabs of brown, patches of green, and bountiful blue, the photo became an instant classic.

The photo's beautiful blues highlight a watery world. In fact, more than 70 percent of the planet is covered with the wet stuff. Nearly 97 percent of Earth's water are salty oceans, while the remaining three percent is fresh water.

Just how much water does Earth boast? A mind-boggling amount—more than 326 million trillion gallons. With a whopping 18 zeroes, the figure looks like this: 326,000,000,000,000,000,000. No wonder Earth is true blue!